RAMONA

BEHIND THE SCENES
OF A TELEVISION SHOW

RAMONA

BEHIND THE SCENES
OF A TELEVISION SHOW

WRITTEN BY
ELAINE SCOTT

PHOTOGRAPHS BY
MARGARET MILLER

MORROW JUNIOR BOOKS/NEW YORK

ACKNOWLEDGMENTS

In addition to all of the actors and actresses who appear before the camera and those persons who worked behind the scenes, we want to thank Larry Lancit, Cecily Truett, Hugh Martin, and Kim Todd for all their help during the preparation of this book. Of course, *Ramona: Behind the Scenes of a Television Show* would not even exist without the initial creativity of Beverly Cleary and the guidance of David Reuther. We will always be grateful to them.

Text copyright © 1988 by Elaine Scott
Photographs copyright © 1988 by Margaret Miller
Photographs on pages 78 and 79 courtesy of Marni Grossman.

Printed in the United States of America.   1 2 3 4 5 6 7 8 9 10

Library of Congress Cataloging-in-Publication Data

Scott, Elaine, 1940–
Ramona : behind the scenes of a television show
by Elaine Scott; photographs by Margaret Miller.   p.   cm.
Summary: Uses an insider's view of the making of the ten-part series "Ramona" to depict how a television show is created, from the script adaptation and auditions
to the actual filming and final editing.
ISBN 0-688-06818-9. ISBN 0-688-06819-7 (lib. bdg.)
1. Ramona (Television program)—Juvenile literature. [1. Ramona (Television program)
2. Television—Production and direction.]
I. Miller, Margaret, 1945–   ill.   II. Title.
PN1992.77.R363S36   1988
791.54'72—dc19   87-33313   CIP
AC

This book is lovingly dedicated to
Beverly Bunn Cleary
in appreciation of
the joy she has brought
to readers around the world

CONTENTS

INTRODUCTION

Mention the name "Ramona Quimby," and children all over the world smile. They have gotten to know her and her friends through seven lively stories—translated into many languages—about the pleasures and problems of the Quimby family.

What is it about Ramona that makes her so popular with children? One young reader says, "I like her because she's just like me. She wants to do the right thing, but sometimes she makes mistakes and people laugh. Then she gets embarrassed. But everything always turns out all right in the end. I like reading about Ramona because it makes me feel that my mistakes can turn out all right in the end, too."

Until recently, Ramona was a fictional character in a series of seven books created by author Beverly Cleary. Now, with the help of over

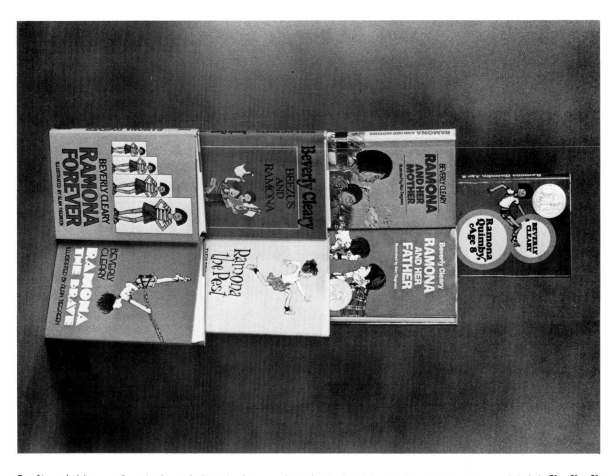

sixty people—producers, directors, camera operators, set and costume designers, makeup artists, lighting and sound technicians, film editors, caterers, and actors—Ramona Quimby has moved from the pages of books to her own ten-part television series, Ramona.

The first television show appeared in the United States in 1929. It was a cartoon, *Felix the Cat*, and it was broadcast from studios in New York City. Today, there are many different kinds of television shows on the air. In addition to the ever-popular cartoons, there are news shows, talk shows, game shows, sporting events, and network specials. However, most television shows, like Ramona, tell a story. Some of the stories on television are serious. Some are funny. Sometimes the stories are both serious and funny, and the show can make us think or cry or laugh—perhaps all three!

As viewers, we must choose what we will watch from among hundreds of television shows on the air each week. Some of the shows are excellent, some just fair, and others aren't very good at all. Nevertheless, at its best, television can be a very fine thing. Like good books and movies and music, good television shows entertain us, educate us, and help us understand ourselves—and each other—a little better.

However, good television shows do not happen magically. A lot of hard work goes into their creation. This book will let you watch as all of the people mentioned above, and more, work together to create the five hours of television that became Ramona.

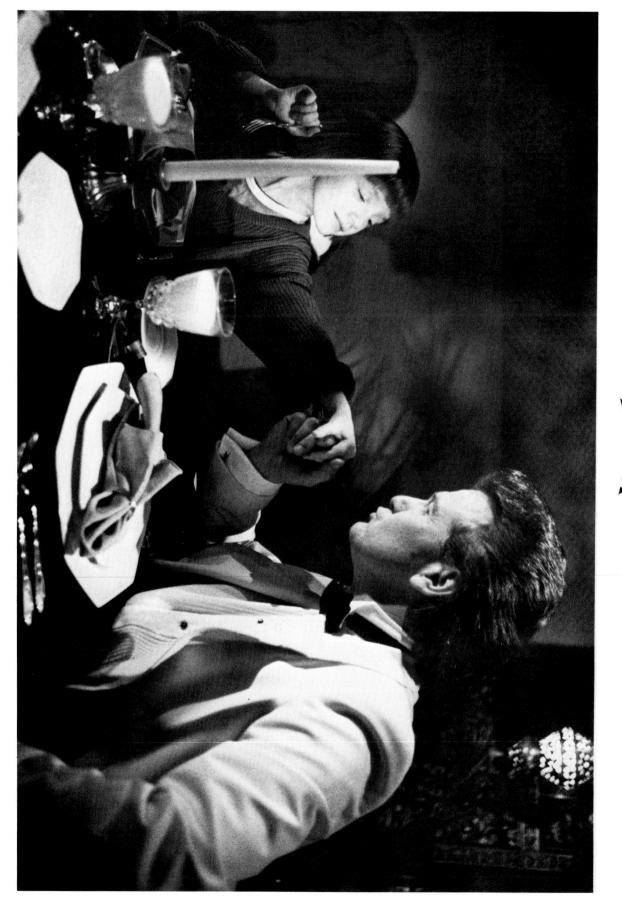

C · H · A · P · T · E · R   O · N · E

BOOKS TO SCRIPTS: HOW DO YOU REWRITE RAMONA?

In a crowded television studio in Toronto, Canada, the Quimby family is seated around a kitchen table, preparing to eat. Mrs. Quimby is dressed like a Middle-Eastern spy; Beezus—in jewelry and veils—looks like a younger version of her mother; Mr. Quimby has on a tuxedo. Only Ramona is dressed in her normal clothes. All of them are discussing the food that is being served for dinner—a kind of "mystery meat" that both girls are eyeing suspiciously.

Anyone who has read *Ramona Quimby, Age 8*, will remember when the girls refuse to eat dinner after they discover their mother is serving tongue. In the book, however, no one was dressed in costume; it was a regular family meal.

What, then, is going on in the television studio? They are supposed

6

to be filming stories about Ramona Quimby, and they are. Nevertheless, these scenes are part of a television script, and while the script is very similar to the book it is taken from, as you have just seen, it is not exactly the same. And the script was not written by Beverly Cleary. Instead, it was written by a screenwriter, or scriptwriter—someone who writes words that will be acted out rather than read silently.

All television shows have scripts. Some scripts begin with the writer's own idea, and the resulting television show is called an original idea or concept. Original ideas often become network specials, shows that are broadcast one time only, like the holiday specials that are so popular. Sometimes scriptwriters come up with their own ideas for a television series. Depending on their length, these shows are called miniseries, limited series, or continuing series, and they can be shown over a period of days or weeks or—in the case of a very popular series like *M•A•S•H*—even years.

However, some of the specials and series you watch are taken from stories that were not written for television at all. These television shows are called adaptations because they have been adapted, or changed, from the original books in order to fit television's needs. *Ramona* is an adaptation from Beverly Cleary's books, and the scene in which Ramona's family is dressed up for dinner is a creation of the scriptwriters, not Mrs. Cleary.

When an author creates fictional characters, as Mrs. Cleary did with the Quimby family, the author and her

publisher "own" those characters. No one else may write about them (other than in a book review or a brief summary) without their permission. People who want to make television shows or plays or movies or stuffed animals or games or *anything* using an author's character must obtain permission to do so from the author and publisher. When they get that permission, the producers will say they bought the rights to a book. Rights are sold, just like any kind of merchandise, and in this case the rights to the books about Ramona Quimby were purchased by Larry Lancit and Cecily Truett. They are the owners of Lancit Media Productions, a television production company that created, among other award-winning shows, *Reading Rainbow.*

Cecily Truett wanted to make a television series from these books because, as she said, "Ramona is a fresh and everlasting and appealing character. There is something about her life, with its problems and its pleasures, that applies to all of us at any age. And, without question, when we interviewed children about their favorite books, they all mentioned Ramona. She was *definitely* the most popular character of all."

Cecily and Larry bought the rights to only three of the books that Mrs. Cleary has written about the Quimby family. Cecily said, "I wanted to keep Ramona at approximately the same age throughout the series, so we bought the rights to the books where Ramona is about 8 years old—*Ramona Forever, Ramona and Her Mother,* and *Ramona Quimby, Age 8.*"

After the rights were purchased, Larry and Cecily asked Hugh Martin to come to work on this project with them. Hugh had worked on some well-known Public Broadcasting System (PBS) shows, such as *Mr. Rogers' Neighborhood*, where he was the producer and director. Because of his experience, Cecily and Larry knew that Hugh would have good ideas for *Ramona*. However, his first response surprised them.

"The books are wonderful," Hugh explained, "but an awful lot of the action goes on in Ramona's head—it's what she's thinking that often makes them funny. I

wasn't sure how to bring that to television. After all, it's hard to film somebody's thoughts!"

Hugh was right. Authors have a certain advantage over scriptwriters because authors can tell their readers what their characters are thinking and feeling. Because television is something people watch instead of read, scriptwriters and directors have to *show*, rather than *tell*, how the characters feel. Hugh, Cecily, and Larry worked with the scriptwriters to develop the fantasies that show Ramona's thoughts—for example, the one described at the beginning of this chapter where she imagines that her mother is the spy Mata Hari and her father is James Bond.

As he talked about how the show developed, Hugh said, "Once the fantasy concept was in place, I knew we had a winner. I liked the Quimby family, and I like stories about family relationships. We need more of that kind of story on television, and I really wanted to work to make that possible."

Next, Hugh, Larry, Cecily, and the scriptwriters thought about the problem of turning the books into television shows. They asked themselves the question, "How do you rewrite Ramona for television?"

One part of the answer was, "You ask Beverly Cleary for some help."

Mrs. Cleary did not want to write the scripts herself, but she did have the right to approve the scripts before they were filmed. In addition, she agreed to work as story consultant, which meant that she would help the

scriptwriters adapt her books for television. It takes a special kind of writer to take the words in an author's book, change them into a television script, and make the script sound as if the original author had written it. Although most books are written by one author, most television shows are written by several scriptwriters.

The work of creating the scripts for *Ramona* began at a story conference at the PBS offices in New York City. Mrs. Cleary met there with the scriptwriters to answer their questions about the Quimbys—after all, no one knows that family better than she!

"I need to know more about the Quimbys—especially Bob. For example, where did Mr. Quimby live when he was a little boy?" The man asking that question leans forward in his chair and waits for Mrs. Cleary to answer. The scriptwriters—Mark Eisman, Mark Saltzman, Ellen Schecter, Ellis Weiner, and Newbery-award winner Sid Fleischman—pick up their pencils, getting ready to take notes on her answer.

Beverly Cleary, a Newbery-award winning author herself, nods her head and smiles. All good authors understand the importance of knowing characters well. They often create "histories" for their characters as if the characters were actual people. Beverly Cleary is happy to share the history she has created for Bob Quimby.

"Why, he grew up in the country. He was raised by his grandmother—in a small town." She pauses for a moment, carefully choosing what she is going to say next. "His grandmother was a strong woman, but she

said all those . . . those *boring* things." Mrs. Cleary rolls her eyes and laughs when she says this, and everyone around the table laughs, too, remembering boring quotes like "Every kettle must rest on its own bottom." When the laughter stops, she continues, as if she were talking about an old friend. "He was an only child . . . but he had a dog." She stops to think about Mr. Quimby's childhood a bit more. "His grandmother gave him paper to draw on," she says; then—almost as an afterthought—she adds, "and Ramona worries about him. She's daddy's girl."

Pencils race across paper as the scriptwriters take notes on everything Mrs. Cleary says. She knows her characters' past, she knows what they are thinking and worrying about right now, and she even peeks at their future. At this morning's meeting, she hints that Beezus "may grow up to be a nurse." This kind of information helps the scriptwriters get to know the Quimby family better, and the better they know the family, the better the scripts will be.

When you read a book by Beverly Cleary, you can probably tell it has been written by her, even if the cover has been torn off. All authors have their own style—a way of saying things that is uniquely theirs. However, since television shows are often the work of more than one writer, you have more than one writing style in all those scripts—and that can be a problem. Beezus can't call Mrs. Quimby "Mother" in one story and suddenly start calling her "Mom" or "Mommy" in another; and

Mr. Quimby can't call his wife "Dory" in some of the shows and "Dorothy" in others. There must be consistency in all the episodes. In order to get this consistency, the writers develop something called a "writer's bible," which they rely on for guidance almost like people rely on the scriptures of their religion!

The writer's bible for *Ramona* contains short descriptive paragraphs about all the characters in the series—what they look like, what they call each other, how they dress. The "bible" tells the scriptwriters other things they need to know, too, such as what the inside of the Quimby house looks like. It even includes a rough floor plan, sketched by Beverly Cleary herself. The writers need to know where the rooms in the house are located so that the bathroom and the kitchen will be in the same places in each script! Descriptions of the neighborhood around Klickitat Street, Ramona's school, the Quimbys' car—everything that has anything to do with the stories is included in the writer's bible. All television shows have a writer's bible with information similar to this one. These "bibles" help scriptwriters produce television shows that sound as if they were written by one person.

Of course, all good writing requires a lot of rewriting, and professional writers are not exempt from this chore. The scriptwriters will do several drafts of each script, incorporating Mrs. Cleary's suggestions as well as any changes the producers want. There will be many drafts of each script, and even then the final show can differ

---

RAMONA Q.

MAJOR AND SOME SUPPORTING CHARACTER BREAKDOWNS

RAMONA QUIMBY..age 8..... Lively, imaginative, naive, determined, hair twirler, bangs blower, knuckle chewer. Although life for her is filled with questions, concerns and disappointments, she embraces it to the fullest. Demands accuracy from everyone as she struggles to understand the complicated world. Mumbles to herself. Takes after her father, loves feeling close to her mother. Has flash fantasies, sees herself in 5-second vignettes.

BEEZUS QUIMBY.. age 12.... Gangly, self-conscious, endearing, phone talker. On the threshold of adolescence and sensitive to all of its trials and tribulations. Always in the mirror and dissatisfied with what she sees. Takes after her mother. Conservative, romantic. Her real name is Beatrice after her Aunt.

DORRIE QUIMBY...30-35..
(Dorothy) Serious, sensible one in the family. Usually unflappable. Slight in stature; straight dark hair; somewhat tired in appearance. The major bread-winner who juggles her job as a secretary in a doctor's office with the neverending obligation as a full-time mother. Affectionate, devoted to her family and supportive of her husband Bob. Good ol' Dorrie.

BOB QUIMBY...30-35...... A dreamer with a comical flair; an inventor of fun; not having found his proper station in life. Having dropped out of college to have a family (the birth of Beezus) he now struggles with his recent return to academia while maintaining his tedious job as a grocery store check-out clerk. Frustrated artist. Seeking to improve his lot through his artistic talent. But does he really have any? Dark-haired, an orphan raised by his grandmother who gave him a lot of boring advice which he spouts to the family. The perfect man to go ice skating with; slim, agile, good physical shape.

from the final script because of last-minute changes made by the director.

In the United States *Ramona* will be broadcast over PBS, which has no commercials. The scripts for the half-hour shows must fill twenty-eight minutes and forty-eight seconds of air time. (The other seventy-two seconds will be taken up with station breaks and announcements of upcoming shows.) If the scripts were being written for one of the commercial networks, such as NBC or ABC, they would only take up twenty-three minutes of air time. The remaining seven minutes would be taken up with commercials. The writers try hard to make their scripts fill the proper time, but no one knows *exactly* how long a scene will take to perform until it is actually filmed. Generally speaking, one page of script equals approximately one minute of program. However, during the filming, the scripts may have to be shortened by removing some scenes, or lengthened by hurriedly writing short scenes, in order to fill the time precisely.

At the story conference Cecily puts rough outlines of each show on the wall. Then each show is discussed, and new ideas for the scripts come from everyone. Cecily writes each idea on a piece of stick-on paper, and soon the outlines are growing yellow tails. The scriptwriters will use these outlines as they work on their scripts.

In addition to the restrictions of time, the writers also try to write scenes that will eliminate the need for too many actors. For example, the script for the show about

```
                         - -LANCIT MEDIA PRODUCTIONS, LTD.
                                Show #2 - Mystery Meal

BEEZUS rolls her eyes--then--

                    BEEZUS
                I forgot about the rice!

                                                    CUT TO

57A  COOKING MONTAGE SEQUENCE

62  AT THE FRIDGE - BEEZUS

is on her hands and knees, rummaging around. Finally she stands
with a fistful of carrots. She takes them over to the
sink--grimly--and starts scraping. Ramona comes over with the
open cook book.

                    RAMONA
                Here's a good dessert recipe for canned
                pears. I think.

                    BEEZUS
                What do you mean, you think?

                    RAMONA
                It's written in a foreign language. "Sawt
                pears with butter, then add one tibble sip
                jelly in the center of each."

                    BEEZUS
                What?
                (stops scraping, looks at book)
                Oh. "Saute." And it's not "tibble sip."
                That's the abbreviation of tablespoon.
                (resumes scraping)
                Get the jelly out before you start. My home
                Ec teacher says you should assemble all your
                ingredients before you start to cook.

                    RAMONA
                Oh, shut up.

                    BEEZUS
                Ramona! Don't tell me to shut up.

                    RAMONA
                Well don't tell me to assemble all my
                ingredients! All my ingredients are
                assembled all over the place!

63  FINAL MONTAGE: BEEZUS pours peas into simmering chicken and
stirs them in; RAMONA puts butter in pan and pours pears in,
messily; BEEZUS puts peeled carrot sticks into a dish; RAMONS
stirs pears.  BEEZUS pours two glasses of milk.  RAMONA unscrews jar
```

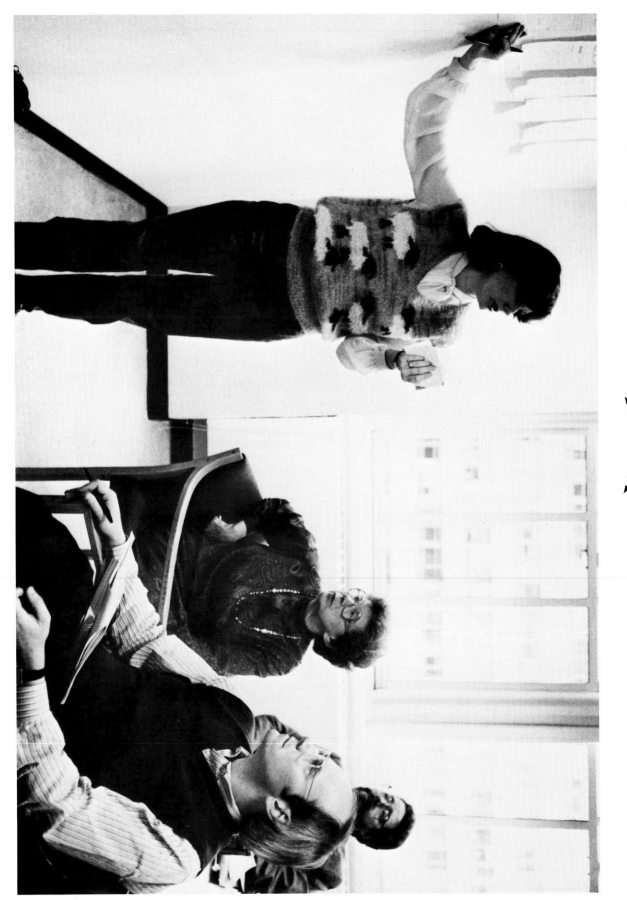

Aunt Bea's wedding originally called for Ramona and her father to be filmed going up and down the street asking various neighbors for flowers to put in the church. When it came time to shoot the scene, the producers realized that it would cost a lot of money to film it that way because actors would have to be hired to play the neighbors, and the entire cast and crew would have to change locations to film it. So the script was changed to show Bob Quimby on the telephone. He looks at his family, who are ready to leave the house, and says, "You go on, I have some calls to make." The scene immediately following shows people arriving at the church carrying armloads of flowers from their yards, and the viewer assumes that's the result of Bob's telephone calls. A small change in this script wound up saving the producers a great deal of money.

Writing television scripts for *any* television show is a complicated, time-consuming business that includes story conferences, writer's bibles, writing, and rewriting. In order to produce the ten scripts needed for *Ramona*, five scriptwriters worked closely with Beverly Cleary, Hugh Martin, and Cecily Truett for nearly a year until, finally, ten of Mrs. Cleary's stories were lifted from the pages of her books and transformed into stories that could—and would—be shown on television screens all over the world.

C·H·A·P·T·E·R   T·W·O

WHO WILL BE RAMONA?

Casting, that is, choosing the actors and actresses who will play the roles, is a very important part of the process of creating a television show. Before *Ramona* was finally cast, actors from all over Canada and the United States had auditioned in hopes of getting parts.

Some of you reading this book may have auditioned for a part in a school play. If you have, you know that an audition is a little like a test. A musician or dancer auditions by performing a short piece of music or a dance. An actor auditions for a play or television show by reading lines from a script.

The casting director is responsible for conducting auditions. Actually, two casting directors worked on *Ramona*. Arlene Berman looked for actors in Canada, and Darlene Kaplan looked in the United States.

Before either casting director even thought about beginning auditions, she sat down and read all of Mrs. Cleary's books about the Quimbys. The casting directors needed to be certain that they knew what the Quimbys, Yard Ape, Howie, Willa Jean, Grandma Kemp, Mrs. Whaley—and all the other characters—were like. As Darlene and Arlene read, they both thought about what the characters looked like—if Mrs. Cleary had described them—and they thought about what they *acted* like, too. For example, everyone who has read the books knows that Ramona is average-sized and has straight hair. She isn't as beautiful as a movie star, but people do say she is "cute" and "the pixie type" (as well as a pest). A very tall, or pudgy, Ramona would not be the right type in this series.

If an actress isn't the right type for a role, there is no point in asking her to audition. However, there are some things about actors and actresses that can be fixed so they can play a role. Hair that is too long can be cut; if it's the wrong color, it can be dyed. Too curly? It can be straightened.

But sometimes the absence of hair can be a real problem. In the books, the character of Uncle Hobart has a beard, so the casting directors looked for an actor with a beard to play the part. Unfortunately, they didn't find one who was "just right." Finally, they found Barclay Hope, the *perfect* Uncle Hobart. But Barclay had no beard, and, since it was late in the filming when he was cast, he didn't have time to grow one. There were hurried

conferences and several attempts at fake beards. Unfortunately, when the best beard was finally finished, it didn't work; it came off Uncle Hobart's chin when he talked! Unexpected things always happen during the production of a television show, and the producers have to be able to cope with them. So after much discussion they decided that—although Uncle Hobart had a beard in the books—on television, he would be beardless.

Beards and hair color can be changed, but some things, like height or skin color, simply can't be changed to suit a particular role. The casting director thinks about all of this before she or he invites various actors and actresses to audition for roles in a show.

The casting directors began the auditioning process by looking through the records they keep of every actor and actress they have ever auditioned for any part in anything! By looking through their records, both Arlene and Darlene were able to find actors who they thought might be right for *Ramona*, and they invited them to audition. They also contacted theatrical agents—people who represent professional actors. They sent the agents a description of the show and the types of actors they would like to audition. The agents looked over this information, and if they represented an actor who they thought could be the right type, the agents sent him or her to the audition. By the time all this work was done, 150 young girls had signed up to audition in New York—just for the part of Ramona! In Canada, Arlene auditioned many more.

These auditions are the first calls, which simply means that anyone who might be right for the part is asked to come read. It took Darlene three days to audition all 150 young "Ramonas" in New York. Out of these, she invited 19 actresses to the "callback" auditions.

Callback auditions are more difficult than the first calls. At callbacks, actors and actresses know they are closer to being chosen than they were the first time they read. They begin to think, "Maybe, just *maybe*, I'll get the part!" Everyone is more nervous this time around.

The New York callbacks are scheduled to last for ten minutes each, but some last longer, and soon the waiting room at the Lancit offices is full of young actresses waiting their turn to audition once again. Most of the girls arrive with their mothers. As they wait, some talk to each other, some rehearse their lines, and some sit quietly. They are nervous, of course, but they are also professionals. They have been to auditions before, and they know that only one person will get the part. If they do not get this role, they will try out for something else. Actors—even very young ones—must be able to take rejection.

Several people are in the audition room, waiting for the callbacks to begin. In addition to Hugh, Cecily, and Larry, two special guests—Beverly Cleary and her husband, Clarence—are here. Darlene has hired Ann Mantel, a reader, to work with the actresses. Ann is a professional actress herself, so she is used to auditions. Depending on the scene the girls are asked to do, Ann

will sometimes read the part of Mrs. Quimby, sometimes she'll be Beezus, and sometimes she's even Mr. Quimby. Although Ann's not auditioning for a part in this series, she will do the best acting she can in order to help the girls who are auditioning. Actors depend on one another. If one does a good job in a part, it helps all the others do a good job, too.

This time a camera operator stands behind a camera, ready to capture everyone's audition on videotape. The producers want to see how all these actresses look on camera. Sometimes a person who is tall in real life can look much smaller on camera. Other people look heavier than they really are. How actors photograph can determine whether or not they get the part. The videotapes are useful, too, when it comes time to make a final decision. Everyone can look at the tape and see how the audition went.

One by one, the girls are called into the room. Anyone who came with them must wait outside. The auditions are done on an individual basis unless the director decides to put girls who are reading for Beezus and Ramona together to see how they react to each other.

As the girls come into the room, they hand Darlene their résumés. A résumé includes a photograph (called a "head shot"), a physical description of oneself (height, weight, color of eyes—things like that), a list of credits (the performances one has done), and training (studies in dance, theater, gymnastics, or voice). In sum, a ré-

sumé includes whatever a producer would be interested in knowing about a performer.

Hugh Martin talks to them briefly, chatting about school, the clothes they have on, or their hobbies. He wants to put the girls at ease before the audition begins. When they are ready, Hugh decides which of the three scenes they have studied he wants them to do. He might tell them a little bit about how Ramona is *feeling* before they begin to read. For example, if he asks an actress reading for Ramona to do the scene in which Picky-Picky dies, Hugh says, "Remember, Picky-Picky was really Beezus's cat, not Ramona's. You won't feel as sad in this scene as Beezus does."

The morning wears on, and each of the actresses has a chance to audition. Sometimes Hugh knows after hearing one scene that the girl will not be right for the part. He will thank her then and she will leave. Sometimes he will ask an actress to read three or four scenes. Hugh is looking for a special quality he calls "direct-ability." He explains what he means by that by saying, "I want someone who can listen—*listen* is really the key word—and understand what she must do in a particular scene. But I don't want a puppet. I want someone who will listen and understand, but who also can bring her own creative ideas to the part." In other words, Hugh is looking for an actress who understands the character of Ramona on her own, but is willing to work with the director in shaping that character.

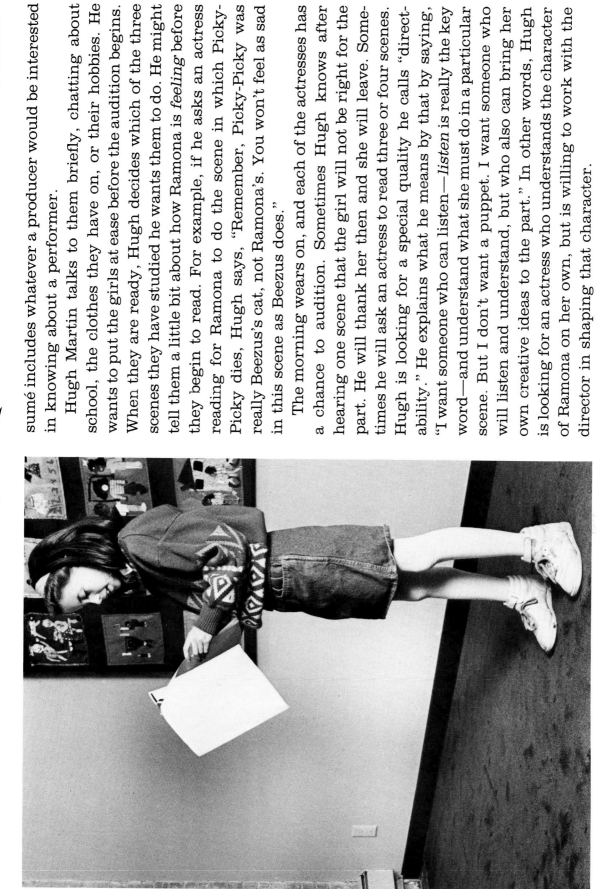

Auditions just like the ones in New York go on in Canada, too, and after months of auditions and callbacks, eight-year-old Sarah Polley of Toronto is finally chosen to play Ramona. Although Sarah is just eight, she has already acted in a number of films and television shows, including *Night Heat* and *Incredible Time Travels of Henry Osgoode*, and she had the lead in the television movie *Heaven on Earth*.

Sarah thought the auditions for Ramona were exciting, but, as she said, "I really didn't think I'd gotten the part when my audition was over. I felt sure that another actress would get it. And then, after my callback, a whole month went by, and I didn't hear anything from anybody, so then I was *positive* I didn't get it."

Although Sarah didn't know it, that month was taken up by sending the tapes of her audition back and forth between New York and Canada so that all the producers could see it. Beverly Cleary saw Sarah's tape, too, and everyone agreed she was the perfect Ramona. She was the "pixie" type, she had read and loved the books about Ramona and understood why Ramona behaved the way she did, and she was a very good actress who took direction well.

Sarah remembered the day she found out she got the part. "One day I came home from school, and as I got off the school bus, my mom was waiting for me. My mom said, 'I have good news. You got the part of Ramona!' I was *so* happy. The next day I went to school. We have the Ramona books in our classroom, and I picked

one of them up, climbed up on a chair, pointed to the book and said, "That's me . . . I'm going to be Ramona!"

Sarah's work with auditions continued after she was cast as Ramona. The producers wanted her to read with the actors who auditioned for the parts of Beezus and Mr. and Mrs. Quimby. In addition to acting talent, the producers were looking for actors who looked right together and seemed to be able to work well together. It was very important that the television Quimby family look and act like a real family.

Eventually, the producers found their Beezus in Lori Chodos, a 12-year-old actress from Toronto. Lori began her career at the age of five, acting in theatrical productions. She had a small part in *The Terry Fox Story*, and a year later, she was cast in *Ramona*. Lori looked right for the part. She had dark hair, like her television "mother," and the two of them looked like a real mother and daughter. But more important, Lori, an honor student at school, was the same kind of responsible, no-nonsense person that Beezus is.

Soon, Barry Flatman and Lynda Mason Green joined the cast as the parents, Dory and Bob. Barry was a wonderful addition to the cast, because besides being a fine actor with dozens of television and film roles to his credit, he was used to working with children at the Home-made Theater, which trained children who wanted to be actors.

Lynda, who plays Dory, had done quite a bit of television and movie work, too. Before *Ramona*, she was in the television miniseries *Amerika*.

Auditions are part of the job for anyone who works in television—even, at times, for stuffed animals! Anyone who has read the books about Ramona knows that a stuffed elephant named (appropriately enough) Ella Funt is one of Ramona's favorite possessions, so the part of Ella Funt was important. The animal had to be just the right type. The prop people gathered several different stuffed elephants together, and while she was visiting the studios in Toronto, Beverly Cleary herself acted

as the casting director.

Mrs. Cleary settled herself comfortably on the sofa in the living room of the television Quimbys and began the audition as the pile of stuffed elephants waited in a basket. "I took this seriously," she said, her voice full of laughter. "I looked at them all. Some were those awful stiff pink-and-green things that look as if they sell for ninety-nine cents in a grocery store. But one was different. It was crocheted, as if someone's grandmother had made it, and it had an ear missing. I don't think the ear was ever *there*, really. And I don't think the child who owned it liked it very much . . . it was *far* too clean to have been played with hard. But it had just the right look about it, and so I chose it. You could say I am the official casting director for Ella Funt."

Darlene Kaplan and Arlene Berman may have auditioned the humans, but Beverly Cleary auditioned the stuffed animals!

Other actors called "extras" will be needed, but they will not be cast for quite a while. The extras have no lines to learn because they do not have speaking parts in the show. Instead, they become the people in crowd scenes, classmates of Ramona's in school, people dining at the restaurant. Usually, the extras in a movie or television show are chosen from among the people who live in the city where the film is being made. In the case of this series, most of the extras will be from Toronto, Canada, because that is the next stop for the cast and crew of Ramona.

C·H·A·P·T·E·R T·H·R·E·E

MONEY! MONEY! MONEY! THE PRODUCERS' PROBLEM

It costs money—lots of it—to produce a television series. Buying the rights to the books is just the beginning of the expense. The scriptwriters must be paid, a studio has to be rented, sets must be designed and built, actors have to be hired to play the parts, there must be a director and a camera operator, and they all need assistants. Then there is makeup and wardrobe, secretaries and accountants, food, and insurance . . . the list goes on and on! In all, approximately sixty people had important jobs in this production, which wound up costing forty-two thousand dollars a day to film. All told, it will cost over three million dollars to create the ten episodes that make up *Ramona*. Raising that kind of money certainly isn't easy, but Larry and Cecily must raise it before they can begin to produce this television series.

Television programs come to our homes over different kinds of television networks. A network is a chain of television stations that is owned by one company. In the United States there are many commercial and cable networks and one noncommercial network. Commercial networks make money by selling advertising time on the air; cable-television networks make money because people subscribe to their service, just as they would to a newspaper or magazine. The Public Broadcasting System is a noncommercial network. It doesn't try to make money, so it doesn't sell advertising time and viewers don't pay to have its programs beamed into their homes. Instead, in order to develop new shows and keep other shows on the air, PBS asks for contributions from its viewers, from businesses, and from the Corporation for Public Broadcasting (CPB), in Washington, D.C.

Larry and Cecily told the people at PBS and CPB about their plans for *Ramona*. PBS immediately gave them some money. And Don Marbury, who is the associate director of the Program Fund at CPB, said, "We've always wanted to see Beverly Cleary's stories on television, so we were glad to help." Eventually, Larry and Cecily discovered that Michel Noll of Revcom Television in Paris, France, and Michael MacMillan of Atlantis Films in Toronto, Canada, were interested in becoming part of this project also. Revcom and Atlantis invested money, and between them, will distribute this series to television stations all over the world. Lorimar Productions is another investor; in return for their money, the people

at Lorimar get the rights to sell home videos from the series.

Once the money has been raised, one of the first things that must be decided is how the show will be broadcast. When the television industry was young, practically all shows were aired "live." Live television means viewers see the show on their television sets exactly as it is being performed in the studio—mistakes and all. News programs and special bulletins—along with a very few regularly scheduled network shows, such as NBC's *Today* show—still go on the air live. However, most of the things you see on television now, whether produced locally or by a network, are put on film or videotape. There are obvious advantages to using these processes. For one thing, "do-overs" are allowed. If a mistake is made during filming, the director can call "Cut!" and the scene will be shot again. Also, a program that is filmed or taped can be shown anytime—as soon as it's completed, or many months later.

Ramona was not done live. Nor was it "taped in front of a live studio audience," as so many game shows and sitcoms (short for "situation comedies") are. Instead, *Ramona* was filmed at the Atlantis Studios in Toronto. Filming a television show is more expensive than taping one, but film has definite advantages over tape. The lighting on the set can be adjusted more precisely, thus eliminating shadows and harsh effects. As Cecily Truett pointed out, "Film has a timeless quality about it. It's, well, it's just *prettier* than videotape."

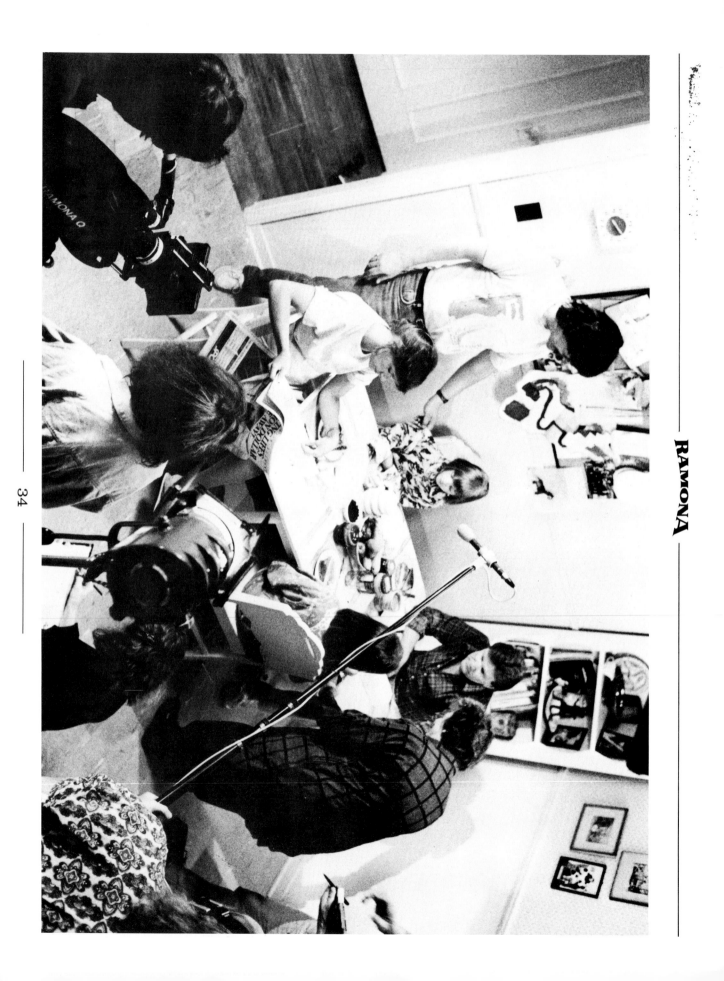

And if the project is filmed, the "set"—the place where the actors actually perform—can be made cozier, too. Shows that are videotaped use three cameras, all rolling at once. This process requires a wide set that is similar to a theatrical stage. The set has to be broad to make room for all those cameras, and its width makes it less realistic than a film set, which can be as small as a real house because only one camera is used.

Shooting on film is often more expensive than shooting on tape, and television producers always worry about money. They worry about raising it, and then they worry about how they're spending it. In order to control how much they spend, the producers set up a budget for the project. Most families have a budget, and all television shows have one. The eighteen-page budget for *Ramona* spells out how much money will be spent for each item that is needed, down to the exact number of hours in a day each lighting technician will work.

"Plan your work, and work your plan" sounds like something Mr. Quimby's grandmother might have said, but that is exactly how television shows eventually get put together. Someone must plan ahead, and someone must see to it that the plans are carried out. The person who does the planning is the line producer, and the person who carries the plans out is the production manager. In the case of *Ramona*, one person is doing both of those jobs. Her name is Kim Todd, and she described her job by saying, "It's like being a mother to fifty people. If the crew doesn't like the food the caterers serve, I hear about it."

Actually, Kim's job involves a lot more than mothering a crew of fifty. As she put it, "In the beginning I'm given an amount of money and the scripts. It's my job to figure out how to get the best quality show for the amount of money we have."

One of the first things Kim does is prepare a storyboard, so the shows can be filmed as quickly and efficiently as possible. A storyboard is prepared by putting information about every scene on strips of paper that can be slipped into clear pockets on a leather-bound "board." At first, the strips are laid out in sequence—that is, they are laid out exactly as the series will be shown on television, beginning with the first scene of the first show and ending with the last scene of the final episode.

A glance at each strip tells—among other things—who is in the scene and where it takes place, whether it's day or night, inside or outside. For example, one glance at a particular strip on the board tells Kim that Picky-Picky is in the scene, it's an interior, which means the action is taking place inside rather than outside, and the time is evening.

As Kim glances over the storyboard, she sees that Picky-Picky also appears in other scenes later in the series, and he will be inside the house then, too. Hiring cats costs money, so it's more efficient to film all those scenes in the house at once, when the lighting is all set up for it. The second assistant director, Frank Siracusa,

pulls all the strips that have Picky-Picky in the house and rearranges them on the board so that all these scenes can be filmed in one day. The same process is repeated with all the actors, grouping scenes together to make the best use of time and money.

After everyone is finished working with the storyboard, a shooting schedule is made. The shooting schedule tells, among other things, exactly which scenes from which scripts will be shot on each day, how many pages of script will be shot, whether the filming will take place at the studio or on location, and the actors who will be needed. This television show will be filmed out of sequence, which means that unlike a stage production, the action will not be performed in the correct order—things may be topsy-turvy. For example, Dory Quimby could be six months pregnant in one scene filmed in the morning and not pregnant at all in a scene filmed that afternoon. (Lynda will wear different kinds of apronlike padding under her clothes that will make her gradually look more and more pregnant as the shows go on.)

Filming out of sequence calls for hard work on the actors' part. They must be able to switch emotions quickly—perhaps crying over Picky-Picky's death in the morning and then enjoying a sinkful of toothpaste in the afternoon. Nevertheless, the actors are professionals, and they are expected to be able to produce whatever emotion the script calls for whenever it calls for it.

After working with the scripts and the storyboard, Kim decides that preproduction—the work that takes place before actual filming begins—should last four weeks and production—the actual filming itself—should last ten weeks. She plans to break those ten weeks into two five-week stretches, with a week off in between for rest and relaxation.

As she looks at this schedule, Kim says, "If we work nine hours a day, five days a week, we'll get through on time." In television work, time is, indeed, money.

Ramona Productions Inc.
65 Heward Ave. Bldg C.
Toronto, Ont. M4M 2T5
(416) 462-0140

RAMONA
CALL SHEET# 19

PRODUCER/PRODUCTION MANAGER:
KIM TODD
DIRECTOR: RANDY BRADSHAW

DATE: THURSDAY, APRIL 30, 1987   LOCATION DAY
**401 West ramp off DVP is closed.

UNIT CALL: 0800 - Unit
0730 - MU/H/WRDRB

UNIT REPORT TO: #1) Yvonne Public School
36 Yvonne Cresc - 241-1896
(SEE MAP)

SUNRISE: 0613   SUNSET: 0819

WEATHER: Partly cloudy, gusty winds
High +10   Low +1

SCRIPT#-SCENE	SET/DESCRIPTION	D/N	CAST	PGS	LOC.
#1-2C	EXT. SCHOOL Establish	D-1	1, Extras	1/8	#1 (Playground)
#1-13	EXT. SCHOOL Call me Squeakerfoot	D-1	1,8,9 Extras	4/8	#1 (Playground)
#1-6	INT. CAFETERIA Egg whacks	D-1	1,8,9,10, 11,12,13, 14,15,31 Extras	1 1/8	#1 (2nd Floor)
#1-6B	INT. CAFETERIA Ramona sent to office	D-1	1,8,9,10, 11,12,13, 14,15,31 Extras	1 1/8	#1 (2nd Floor)
TARGET OF OPPORTUNITY-----					
#7-4	INT. CAFETERIA Tough pot-roast sandwich	D-1	1,8,9,10, 11,12,13, 14,15,31 Extras	5/8	#1 (2nd Floor)
			TOTAL PAGES = 4 5/8		

ARTISTE	CHARACTER	P/U	MU/H/WRDRB	ON SET	LOC#
SARAH POLLEY	1. RAMONA	0710	0800	0830	#1
MARLOW VELLA	8. YARDAPE	0715	0800	0830	#1
BOBBY BECKEN	9. HOWIE	0715	0800	0830	#1
KERRY SEGAL	10. MARSHA	0650	0900	0930	#1
NICOLE LYN	11. SUSAN	N/A	0900	0930	#1
BEN BARRETT	12. TOMMY	N/A	0900	0930	#1
HARVEY CHAO	13. TEACHER IN CAFETERIA	N/A	0900	0930	#1
LISA JAKUB	14. GIRL #1	N/A	0900	0930	#1
MICHELLE WESNALDI	GIRL #2	N/A	0900	0930	#1
GILLIAN SUSSMAN	GIRL #3	N/A	0900	0930	#1
ROBBIE BUDD	15. BOY #1	N/A	0900	0930	#1
NATHAN ADAMSON	BOY #2	N/A	0900	0930	#1
ALVIN CHAU	BOY #3	N/A	0900	0930	#1
RICHARD OJHA	BOY #4	N/A	0900	0930	#1

C·H·A·P·T·E·R   F·O·U·R

CREATING KLICKITAT STREET

There really *is* a Klickitat Street. But it's in Portland, Oregon, and this television series is being filmed in Toronto, Canada. And there really is a house that looks like Ramona's house . . . it's the house Mrs. Cleary grew up in, but it, too, is in Portland. And the school that Ramona attends? You guessed it, there's one that looks just like it . . . in Portland.

Somehow, somewhere in Toronto, someone has to find a house, and a school, and a neighborhood that looks like the ones in Oregon. This is the job of the location manager, John Calvert.

Armed with photographs of Mrs. Cleary's childhood home in Oregon, John spends weeks and weeks driving around the neighborhoods of Toronto. The house has to be within an hour's drive of the studio

to keep transportation costs down, and it has to be on a tree-lined street. To complicate matters further, John says, "Everyone wanted the house to have wood siding, and there simply aren't many frame houses in Toronto—ours are mostly brick. And then, when I did find frame houses, they weren't on tree-lined streets."

Finally he finds the perfect house on the right kind of tree-lined street. All it needs is a fresh coat of paint and a few repairs. The producers agree to do these things and, in addition, pay a fee to the owners in exchange for their permission to film there.

While the repair work is going on, Peter Grundy, the art director, measures both the interior and the exterior of the house carefully. Then he takes pictures of it and the other houses on the street. Using the measurements and the pictures, he draws up plans for what will become the set in the studio. In the case of Ramona, the set includes the Quimby house and everything that's in it.

Before the set construction begins, the studio is one vast, empty space. It measures eighty by one hundred feet, and it is thirty feet high up to the grid. The grid is a series of poles that hang from the ceiling and intersect in a boxlike pattern over the set. Many of the lights that will be needed for filming will be hung from this grid.

Steven Bratton has worked with Peter Grundy before, and now Peter asks him to be the construction manager on this project. First the crew lays a floor over the one in the studio, and then they begin to put up the walls.

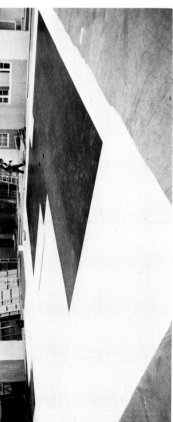

Within two weeks, Steven and his five assistants have reconstructed and installed the Quimby house—right inside the Atlantis studios.

Oh, the house on the set is minus a few things, such as a roof. But water runs when a faucet is turned on, and the fireplace can have a real fire in it. The walls that are in place "blow away" (television talk that means that they can be easily removed) so the camera and crew can film action that takes place in cramped spaces, like the Quimbys' bathroom. And even though the set is inside the studio, if the script calls for a rainy day, "rain" will drip down the windows—thanks to small hoses tacked along the window's outside edges.

For some scenes, the camera will look out the set's windows, so Peter must do something to make the view from the set's windows onto the imaginary Klickitat Street exactly the same as the view from the windows of the house John found tucked away on a Toronto street. The backyard of the real house has a giant tree in it, so that tree is reconstructed in the studio out of lumber, chicken wire, and plastic. Two-by-fours form the skeleton of the tree, and chicken wire gives it a shape; then thin sheets of plastic called Vacuform are heated and formed into texture that looks like the tree's bark. Artificial leaves top the tree, while artificial grass, plants, and flowers "grow" on the ground. A swing set and lawn chairs complete the picture of the Quimbys' backyard.

Last, but certainly not least, scenic artist Nick Kosonic paints a giant backdrop thirty feet high and three hundred and fifty feet around. Nick is used to this kind of work . . . he just finished doing the backdrop for the movie *The Fly*. For *Ramona* he looks at the pictures of the street where the real house stands and duplicates all those houses, trees, and shrubs on the backdrop. Now, no matter where the camera focuses, it will see parts of Ramona's neighborhood.

When construction on the set is finished, walls are painted and wallpaper is hung. Then the set is "dressed" with comfy, well-used furniture . . . just the sort the Quimbys would have. The property master brings in pictures for the walls, books for the bookcases, food for the refrigerator, toothpaste for the medicine cabinet—all the things people normally have in their homes. These items are called props, which is short for "properties." Thanks to the prop people, artwork typical of the kind Ramona would do is displayed on the refrigerator and in her room. In fact, when Beverly Cleary visited the set, she pronounced it "just right" and commented that even the clock on the mantel was exactly like a clock she had had on her mantel at home.

Finding locations and building sets are all part of preproduction. So is assembling the wardrobe for the actors. Maya Mani is in charge of this, and like the casting director, the first thing Maya did was read all the books about Ramona. Since the Quimbys do not have much extra money, Maya decided to shop for clothes at stores like Woolco and J. C. Penney. She even raided her children's closets for items that they might have outgrown.

Maya pays attention to many tiny details, too. As she says, "I thought Ramona would have very few things that really fit her. Her clothes would either be too big, because they were new and Mrs. Quimby wanted her to have room to grow into them, or a bit too small, because she was growing out of them."

The clothes not only have to look right, they have to work right, too. One of the scripts calls for Aunt Bea to wear ski clothes, but her outfit has to be changed when the sound experts say the swishing sound of nylon ski clothes is far too noisy for the sensitive television microphones.

Within three weeks Maya has assembled everything the cast will wear—pajamas, shoes and socks, shirts, and dresses. The clothing she can't buy—such as Mrs. Quimby's Mata Hari spy outfit—she makes herself. Maya even makes a patch of "scrambled eggs" for Sarah to wear during a fantasy sequence in which she worries that hot water during a shampoo will cook the raw egg that is in her hair.

Once it's assembled, the wardrobe is hung on racks in the wardrobe room, waiting to be used. The wait will not be long, because preproduction is over and production is about to begin.

C·H·A·P·T·E·R   F·I·V·E

LIGHTS! CAMERA! ACTION!

Before filming could begin, Sarah needed to have her long blonde hair cut and dyed a light brown to look like Ramona's. Then she was ready for the hair and makeup test. There is no studying for this test . . . it is simply a way to determine how Sarah and the other actors look on film and to make any necessary adjustments in their hairstyles and colors or their makeup before actual filming begins.

After the hair and makeup tests are completed, Jan Green, a dialogue coach, arrives at the studio to work with Sarah and Lori. Both girls have a tremendous number of lines to memorize, especially Sarah, who appears in practically every scene of the series. Explaining how she works, Sarah says, "I go over the lines at home at night, if I'm not too tired, and sometimes my mother listens to me say them."

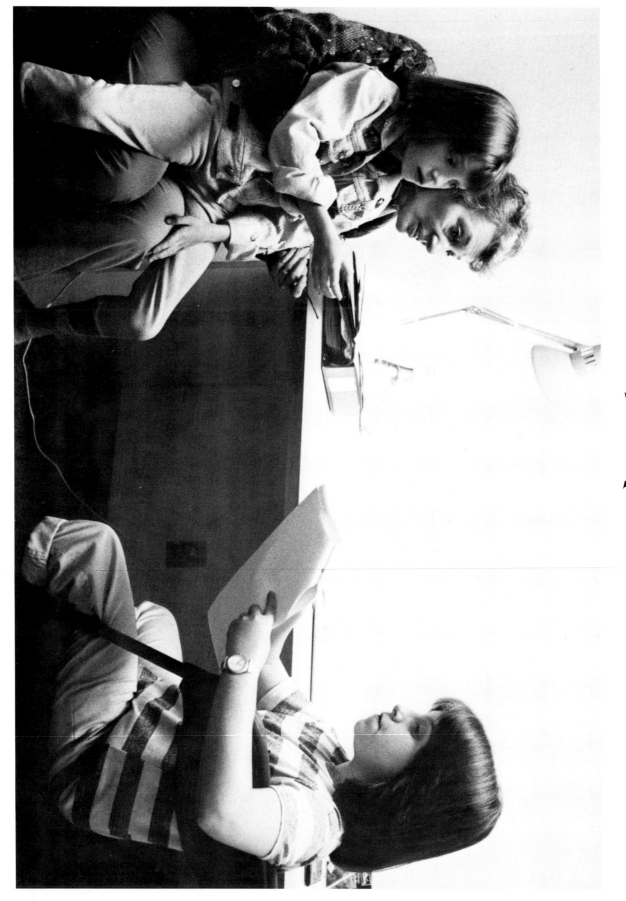

But most of the memorizing is done each day at the studio. Jan helps by "running lines" with both Sarah and Lori. As the girls practice, Jan listens and gives suggestions. In one instance, she says to Sarah, "Be a bit more spontaneous when you say that line."

Sarah looks puzzled and asks, "What does *spontaneous* mean?"

Then Jan pulls Sarah onto her lap and explains, "*Spontaneous* is something you do without thinking about it. If you hit me, and I hit you right back before I think about it, I'm being spontaneous." Jan takes a playful poke at Sarah.

Sarah and Lori laugh at this example and go back to the job at hand—going over lines until they are memorized and talking with Jan about how their characters would be feeling during a particular scene. Jan helps the girls talk about the sadness people feel when a pet dies, or the jealousy that children sometimes feel when a new baby comes. This kind of coaching will help them both have their lines "camera ready" when the director calls them to the set.

Two days before filming begins, the entire Quimby "family" gathers at the studio to rehearse. Rehearsing usually involves practicing something over and over again until you get it just right, but television rehearsals are different. At first, the actors will just read over all ten scripts, from beginning to end, so they can get used to the entire story that the series will tell. In addition to getting used to the scripts, Sarah and Lori and their television "parents," Barry Flatman and Lynda Mason Green, use this rehearsal time to get to know each other a bit better. Just for fun, they all play a game called "Quarters." They lie down, put quarters on the tips of their noses, and then try to see who can wiggle the quarter off first—no hands allowed! It's not as easy as it appears!

Reading the scripts together, being silly, talking and laughing, help the actors feel comfortable with each other, and soon the four of them begin to feel like a real family, which is just what the producers want. Now their performance will be realistic. The actors top off their rehearsal time by wandering through their "house" on the set, getting used to its nooks and crannies, so it will feel like a real home to them when it comes time for the camera to roll.

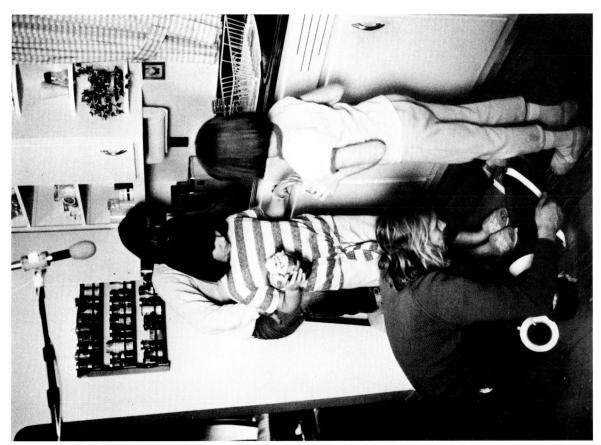

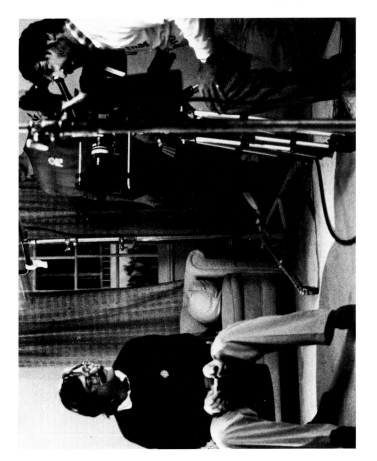

Finally, the actual filming is ready to begin. But before any scene can be shot, the director, Randy Bradshaw, and the director of photography, Doug Kiefer, must work together to block it. As you watch a television show you see the actors standing, sitting, and generally moving around the set in a way that looks very natural. In truth, every move the actors make is carefully planned. This process is called blocking. Doug and his camera follow the actors around as they move through the scene. He tries photographing them from different angles—shooting down on them, shooting up at them, sometimes shooting at their level. Randy also decides whether he wants a close-up or a shot taken from farther away. Once a decision on each shot is made, an assistant will put a strip of tape or a sandbag, called the actor's mark, on the floor out of the range of the camera. Marks help the actors stand or stop exactly where they should as they film a scene.

The lights that illuminate the set can be adjusted in hundreds of different ways. During blocking, Doug decides how much light he wants and where he wants it, and then he asks the lighting gaffer, Gary Phipps, to trim the lights accordingly. The gaffer is the person who is in charge of the lights, and the lighting grip is the person who helps the gaffer by moving the lights from place to place.

When a camera operator talks to a gaffer, it is almost as if they were conversing in an alien language.

"Barn-door that inkie off the wall, will you, Phipps?" asks Doug, and Phipps turns to his grip and asks him to climb up on a kitchen cabinet to adjust a black reflector (that does indeed look a bit like a barn door) over the "inkie," a 750-watt light, until the light shines exactly where Doug wants it.

By carefully moving the reflectors, the gaffer can create shadows on walls and take shadows away from faces. Different-colored filters, called gels, can be placed over the lights to give the scene a different mood. Filters placed over the lens of the camera can also change the lighting. For example, a special filter on the camera can

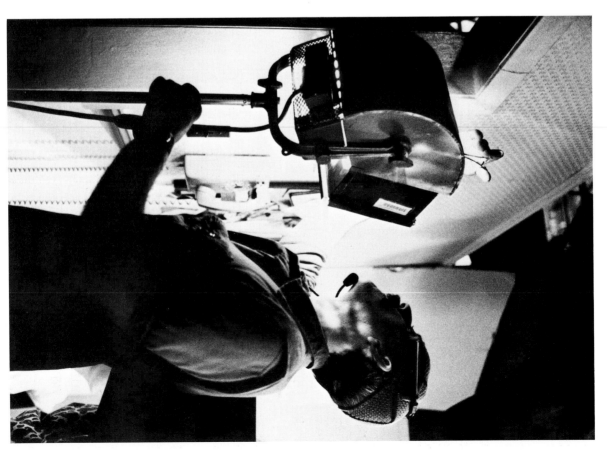

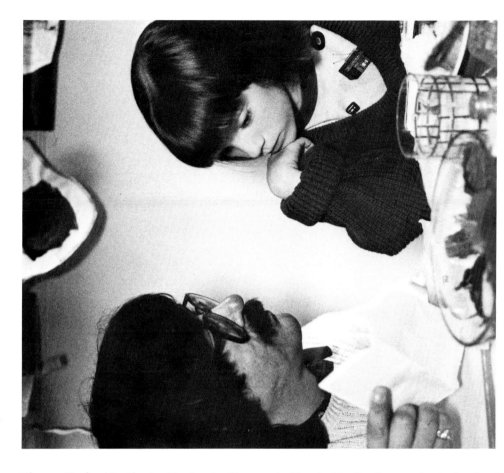

change the ordinary flame of a candle into a star-shaped glow.

Once a scene is blocked and lit properly, the actors are ready to rehearse it. By this time, they have their lines memorized, and they move around the set as if it were a real "take"—television talk for the moment when the cameras actually start to take a picture. During rehearsal, the director may make suggestions on ways the scene could be improved. After one rehearsal is finished, Randy walks on the set, leans down, and whispers in Lori's ear, "That was good, now let's try the line a little more angry, okay?"

Sometimes Randy just tries to encourage his actors. Because they are both young, Sarah and Lori often get tired in the afternoon after a long morning of filming. It's hot under those lights, and it can be boring saying the same lines over and over again. Before a take late in the day, Randy smiles at them and says, "Okay, lots of energy now," and the girls perk up.

Randy also relays instructions for other people on the set. If the sound mixer can't hear the actors properly, or thinks that the knives and forks clatter too loudly when they're on the kitchen table, he will let the director know. Then Randy will tell everyone to put his or her utensils down *lightly*. Because children have softer voices than adults, occasionally Sarah and Lori have to be "wired for sound"—that is, they have to have wires and microphones taped to their bodies, so their voices will be heard.

This morning the cast and crew will work on an as-

sortment of scenes that take place in the Quimby kitchen. As soon as the actors have taken their places and rehearsed their lines a few times, the crew is ready for the first take of the day.

During blocking and rehearsals, everyone relaxes a bit. They laugh and joke and chat with everyone on the set. But a take is a different matter. Takes are serious business, and there is little time for joking. All takes begin with a sequence of commands issued by the first assistant director, Erika Zborowsky, after the director has given her the nod that he is ready to begin the shot. Not surprisingly, the first command is "QUIET!" Instantly, everyone on the set settles down because every noise, even the sound of a footstep, can be picked up by the boom, a sensitive microphone that is held above the actors, out of sight of the camera.

"Final touches!" Erika calls out, and the makeup and wardrobe personnel make any final adjustments the actors need. Someone's nose may be shining too much, and the makeup person will give it a dusting of powder. Ramona's shirt may have come untucked, and the wardrobe mistress will retuck it. If a strand of hair is out of place, the hairdresser puts it back where it belongs.

When final touches are completed, Erika yells, "Bell up!" A buzzer sounds and a red light over the studio door flashes on, warning everyone not to come in while filming is going on.

"Roll sound!" she says.

The sound mixer answers, "Speed," which means his

sound recorder is up to speed and ready to begin taping the voices of the actors.

"Roll camera!" Erika says, and Doug begins to film.

"Mark it!" Erika says, and someone snaps the slate in front of the camera. The slate contains important information about the scene that is being filmed, information that will help the film editor when it is time to put all the scenes together to make a finished episode. The snapping sound the slate makes is a helpful cue to the sound editor, who must coordinate the sound tape with the film.

Finally, the director speaks. "Action!" Randy says, and while everyone else on the set is as silent as a stump, the actors begin to perform.

After the master shot—the first shot of the scene—is finished to Randy's satisfaction, Erika will call out, "Check the gate." The assistant camera operator will then check to be certain that nothing—not even a speck of dirt or a hair—has gotten into the gate where the film passes in front of the lens of the camera. Anything at all would show up on the completed take, ruining it.

When the assistant camera operator answers, "Gate is clean," Erika gives the command, "turning around." Then the dolly grip, the person in charge of moving the camera, slowly rolls it (and Doug, who is literally riding on it) into another position, and the entire scene is filmed again from a different angle.

If all the scenes were filmed from just one angle, the final show would not be interesting to watch. To make

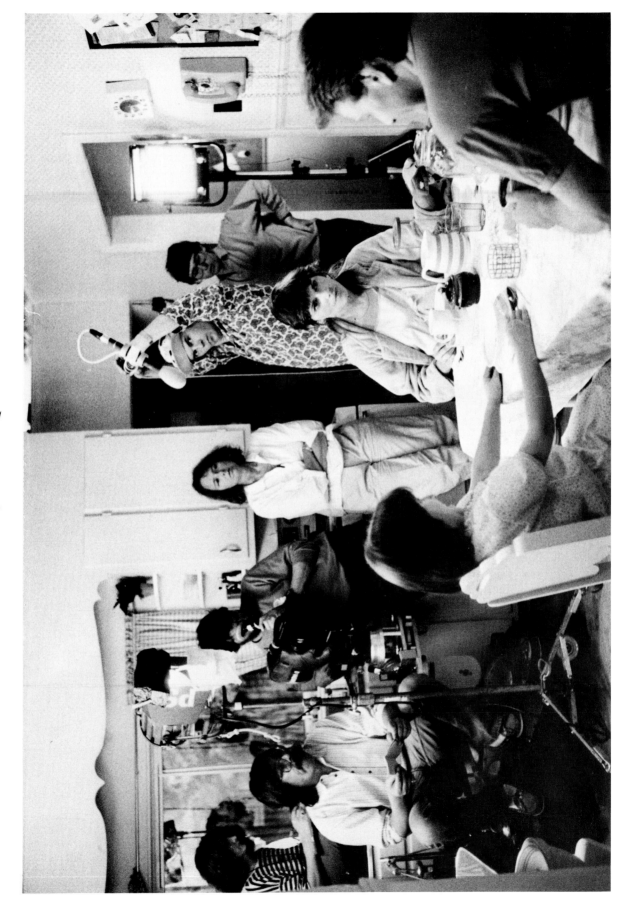

it more interesting, some shots are made to show the actor who is speaking, and others are made to show the reaction of other actors to what has just been said. Occasionally, the camera will pan around a room or look out a window. Filming from different angles adds reality to a scene and allows the viewers to feel as if they were in the room, right along with the Quimbys.

Filming like this is very tiring for the actors. Again and again they must say the same lines, while the camera catches the action from a different angle. When they finally appear on your television screen, they should look as if the lines were being delivered for the very first time. In reality, it will take an hour of this kind of filming to produce just one minute of the show you will finally see on your television screen.

As each take is finished, a person responsible for continuity comes on the set and takes Polaroid pictures of everything, from how the table was set to what kind of food is on the plates. Since the series is being filmed out of sequence, continuity also takes pictures of the actors as they finish each scene. A glance at the pictures tells the prop people exactly how the table was set and the kinds of food that were on the plates the last time this scene was filmed. The hairstylists and wardrobe people can duplicate the way the actors looked during the scene— right down to the time on their watches.

During the filming, Sarah begins to lose a tooth. Everyone around her is worried that the dangling tooth is hurting her, but Sarah says, "I'm not worried about

my tooth. I'm worried about continuity . . . I'm afraid when it's out, the hole in my mouth will show and we'll have to shoot those scenes all over again." As it turned out, Sarah's missing tooth doesn't show, so none of the scenes have to be reshot. But actors like Sarah worry about continuity as much as they do about pain!

Although the four Quimbys sitting around their kitchen table is all the television audience will see, in reality during filming nineteen people are hovering around them, just out of camera range. It is very hard for actors to ignore all these people and concentrate on delivering their lines correctly, take after take. Some takes are repeated a dozen times! The days are long—beginning with makeup at 7:00 A.M. and ending, for Sarah and Lori, at 5:00 P.M. (The other members of the cast and crew work much longer.) The girls try to relax when they can, so they won't tire out too quickly, and Jan is on the set to go over lines between takes and offer an encouraging word or two when she thinks it's needed.

When the morning's kitchen scenes are finally finished, the property crew begins to dress the set for the James Bond fantasy scene. They install a ceiling fan, potted palms, and a filigree screen to transform the no-frills Quimby kitchen into a Middle-Eastern cabaret.

The rest of the cast leaves to change their costumes and makeup, which (along with the change in the set) will indicate that the action in this scene is going on in Ramona's imagination. As they leave, Laurel Bres-nahan, the girls' tutor, comes for Sarah.

"Time for school," she says with a smile, and Sarah follows along. For the next half hour or so, Sarah's dressing room will become a schoolroom as she dutifully does her homework. Laurel will work with Lori sometime later in the day, because both girls must try to get in at least three hours of tutoring a day. Of course it's not all work and school on the set. There are brief moments when Sarah can play a game of cards with one of the crew or clown with Lori.

Sounds of laughter float from behind the closed doors

of the makeup and wardrobe rooms. Soon Barry walks out, looking far more dapper than the Bob Quimby character who entered a few minutes earlier. Every hair is carefully combed into place, and he is dressed in a tuxedo. There is more laughter and the sound of jingling bells in Lynda's dressing room. Soon she emerges, and Dory Quimby has been transformed into a belly-dancing spy named Mata Hari! Lori is dressed up, too, and the cast reassembles on the set, ready to shoot the fantasy sequence.

"Who are you?" Ramona asks her father, who answers that he is "Bond . . . James Bond." He then proceeds to introduce her to his companion, Mata Hari. Ramona asks "Mata Hari" what kind of meat they are having, and the answer is a mysterious "something we have never had before." Lynda delivers this last line in a thick accent, which makes everyone at the table (and the rest of the crew) burst into laughter.

"Cut!" yells Randy, and all of the action stops. The scene will have to be filmed again.

This is the way the entire series will be put together, scene after scene, take after take, inside the studio and away from it. Although a lot of the action in this series takes place in the Quimby house, some of it takes place at Ramona's school and other places, like the church where Aunt Bea gets married, the restaurant where the family meets the mysterious stranger, and the hospital where Mrs. Quimby has her baby. In order to film these scenes, the cast and crew leave the studio and go on location.

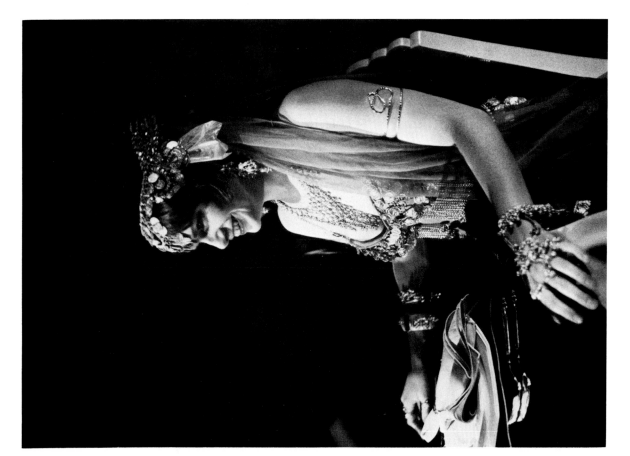

C·H·A·P·T·E·R   S·I·X

AWAY ON LOCATION

Location filming is much more difficult than working in a studio—especially if it is done outside. The dolly grip can roll the camera easily across the smooth floor of the studio, but the camera must roll on a track if the filming is done outside. Otherwise the camera and, therefore, the picture will jiggle and jump around. So a track that looks like a small railroad is quickly laid across the rough pebbles of the school playground where the first day of location filming will begin.

John Calvert, the location manager, had a hard time finding a school to use. It had to be one that was empty because, as John said, "School boards take a dim view of interrupting classes to film a television show." Eventually he located the Yvonne Avenue School. It had been closed because there were not enough children left in the neighborhood to keep it open, and the school board was willing to let the production company rent the building.

The cast and crew arrive at the school at 8:00 A.M. Even though it is daylight, the lighting crew has work to do. Lights have to be set up inside the school for the lunchroom and classroom scenes. And outside on the playground, Phipps, the gaffer, must follow the actors around, holding up a large white shield that reflects natural light off them, just the way Doug Kiefer wants. All this activity is complicated by the weather. Inside a studio, people create the weather. Outside, on location, it's left up to nature, and nature doesn't always cooperate.

A cold north wind blows over the playground at the school the first morning. The crew wear winter parkas but, because the scene is not supposed to take place in winter, the actors have to make do with light jackets.

The temperature is something that no one can control, but John Calvert can do something to control the rain. He can't make nature's rain stop, but he can make rain start in any way he wants . . . from a drizzle to a downpour. Giant rain towers can be moved onto the location. If the script calls for rain and the Toronto weather doesn't cooperate, his towers will.

Now that the crew is working on location, the cast has expanded. Yard Ape, Howie, Marsha, and all of Ramona's school friends are in these scenes, and actors have been hired to fill these roles. Also, plenty of extras are needed to play on the playground, eat in the cafeteria, and be in the schoolroom, and they are hired, too.

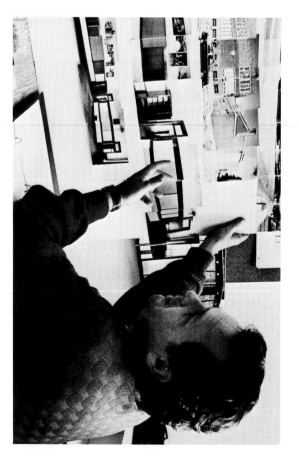

Although extras have no lines, they are still important and must be able to follow instructions.

The first inside scene takes place in the school cafeteria. The real cafeteria in the Yvonne Avenue School is being used as a waiting room for all the extras and their parents, so John Calvert has converted the school's library into Ramona's cafeteria for the filming. The bookshelves have been removed, tables and brightly colored chairs have been installed, stacks of trays sit on serving counters, and colorful posters dot the walls.

As the scene in the cafeteria begins, Sarah and the other actors are all set to crack hard-boiled eggs on their heads, just as Mrs. Cleary described in *Ramona Quimby, Age 8.* Everything is ready. The prop people have four dozen hard-boiled eggs ready to go, and two dozen raw ones. Sarah and the actors who play Howie and Marsha and Yard Ape are ready to work. Randy knows that school cafeterias are busy places at lunchtime, so he calls for a few extras to walk behind Sarah's table carrying trays of food. Five boys and girls are picked from the group of extras and sent to the set.

Erika gives them directions. "All I want you to do is walk behind Howie. Just walk behind him when I signal you, and keep on walking until you are out of the range of the camera. Okay?"

Five heads nod "okay."

"Let's rehearse it once," Erika says, and they do. Now it's time for a take. Randy calls "Action!" and the first four extras walk back and forth behind the actors, just

as they were told. But the fifth extra gets a sudden case of stage fright and refuses to walk at Erika's signal. She signals again and again . . . the cameras are rolling . . . and he shakes his head "no."

"Cut!" yells the director. The young man looks disappointed as he is led back to the large room where all the other extras wait for a chance to be in the show. Quickly, someone else is called to take his place, because making television shows is serious business—even when you are eight years old.

Location shooting began in April when the Toronto weather was cold and blustery. The crew dressed in parkas, gloves, and wool caps; the caterers served hot soup to keep everyone warm. By the time location shooting is almost over in July, the crew have replaced their parkas with shorts and their gloves with sunglasses; lightweight hats protect heads from a sun that beats down on everyone. The caterers serve Popsicles as the cast and crew and all the equipment move to the street in front of Ramona's house to shoot exteriors.

Neighbors pour out of their houses to watch the excitement as the crew set everything up once again. Another fantasy is going to be filmed. In this one, Ramona is worried that her parents will get a divorce after they fight over Dory's pancakes. In her imagination, Ramona sees her house boarded up and her parents packed up, ready to leave. She is alone in her bed, right in the middle of the front lawn!

Soon after the filming of this scene begins, Cecily and Hugh realize that there is not enough script to fill the program's 28 minutes and 48 seconds. They need only a few seconds—not enough to add more lines to the script. Finally Hugh gets an idea. "Let's ask Doug to shoot the scene on the front lawn in slow motion, because slow motion will let us emphasize how worried Ramona is. And the slower action will get us the extra seconds we need."

It is the camera operator, not the actors, who controls the speed of the action; the actors move normally while being filmed. It seems strange, but film that goes through the camera quickly produces slow motion on the screen. The speeded-up camera records more images per second, so when the developed film is shown at normal speed, the action appears to be slowed down. And film that runs slowly through the camera when it is shooting produces action that races across the screen. Hugh wants slow motion, so Doug speeds up the film. Sarah and Lori perform the scene normally, and soon Ramona's dreamy front-yard fantasy is finished.

C·H·A·P·T·E·R   S·E·V·E·N

FITTING ALL THE PIECES TOGETHER

People who take pictures—even snapshots—are eager to get their film developed so they can see what kind of photographs they have. Television producers, directors, and camera operators are no different—they are eager to see what they have, too. Each day, when all the takes of a scene have been shot, the director chooses which of the takes he wants to see right away. If four takes of a scene have been shot, the director might ask to see take one and take four, because he feels they will be the best.

All the film of the day's shooting, called the dailies, is taken to a laboratory every night, where it is quickly developed and returned to the studio the following day. There, an assistant editor works with the takes the director has asked to see, editing them into one piece of film, which is sometimes called a rush because of the rush everyone is in to see it.

Days spent filming television shows are long, and they don't end when the last take of the day is finished and the director says, "That's a wrap for today." At the end of the day, when everyone is very tired, the producers, director, film editor, and camera operator (and any other members of the cast and crew who want to stay) still have work to do. They gather together to watch the rushes of all the different scenes, and everyone talks about which takes of a scene they like best.

"The camera really loves her face in a close-up," says Cecily as she watches the rushes of a scene showing Sarah and Barry talking together on the sofa.

Doug Kiefer, the director of photography, nods his head in agreement, and soon another version of the same scene flashes on the screen.

"That's good, too," someone else says, as the camera takes a different view of the same scene.

Sally Paterson, the film editor, looks pleased. Her job begins now, and she is happy to have good dailies to work with.

Filming a television show is a bit like putting a jigsaw puzzle together. As you know, the episodes are filmed scene by scene, take after take. As film editor, Sally must choose from among all these takes in order to piece a complete scene together.

In order to edit Ramona, Sally uses a Steenbeck editing machine. The Steenbeck has a screen built in so

she can see the film easily, and it has a place to thread the sound tape, too. Sally can view the film with the sound, or without it. The sound track that Sally works with only has the voices of the actors on it. Other sound effects, such as falling rain, cats meowing, or telephones ringing, will be added later. Sally also has a copy of the script with her as she works. In order to edit the film, she must know what has gone on in the scene that comes before the one she is working on, and she must know what will follow in later scenes. Since she will get the takes in the same out-of-sequence order they were filmed in, the script helps her with continuity.

As Sally watches each take flash by on the screen in front of her, she makes a decision as to what must be cut out and what should be left in.

There is a small lever on the Steenbeck that Sally pushes to cut the film at the precise point she wants. She works quickly, cutting and splicing the different takes together until the scene satisfies her. In editing the film, Sally is looking for two things: the performance of the actors and the quality of the picture. Sometimes the acting in one take will be wonderful, but the camera hasn't taken a good picture—the actors might be off in a corner, or the shadow of the boom shows. Sometimes the camera work is lovely, but the performance of the actors isn't up to par. If she can, Sally will piece together good acting and good camera work to come up with a scene that pleases everyone.

the daily rushes are saved, too. There might be something in one of them that Sally or Randy will need later on.

Film editing is part of a process called postproduction, work that goes on after the actual filming. Sally is working while the filming is going on, but her work is still considered part of the postproduction process because she works on completed film.

When all of the story has been shot and the actors have gone on to other jobs, Sally still has work to do. Now she has to choose among all the scenes and put together the complete show. This first edition of the show is called a rough cut. Like a rough draft of a manuscript, the rough cut still needs work, but for the first time, *Ramona* is a television show that begins at the beginning and stops at the end, with all ten episodes in the right order.

Sally shows her rough cut to the producers and the director. Now Randy looks it over and makes any changes he wants. He is making the director's cut. As he edits, he can pick something from the trims to add to the rough cut or he can take something out. Cecily and Hugh go over the film next, polishing and changing it still more. This is the final cut and is very close to what you will see on television. However, as Hugh said, "Nothing is ever cast in concrete until the show goes on the air. The final editing can change things completely."

In fact, in the final editing Hugh and Cecily change the ending of the show where Picky-Picky dies. Origi-

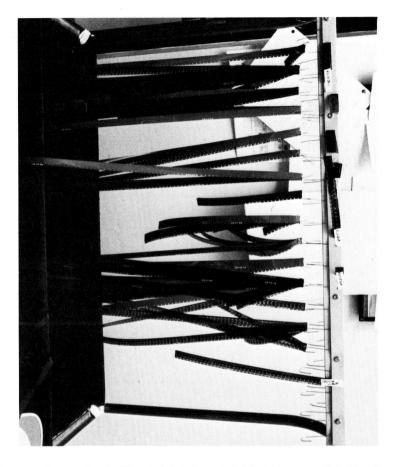

"I join the pieces of film together with ordinary Scotch tape," Sally said. "And I usually discard twelve minutes of film for every minute I use. An eight-hour day of shooting normally produces five or six minutes of usable film."

The trims, film she doesn't use, aren't thrown away. As she works, Sally hangs all the trims by the side of her Steenbeck, just like laundry on a line. The trims are saved in case the director needs to put something back in that Sally took out. The takes that were not part of

nally, the show closed with a conversation between Ramona and Howie about the new baby that was coming. Ramona is not too happy about "its" arrival. Hugh and Cecily want a more upbeat ending, so they choose the scene in which Ramona and her mother hug and Ramona is reassured that she will always have a special place in the middle of her mother's heart. Switching the scenes around is not too difficult, but now some of the lines don't make sense because the scenes were not originally filmed to go together this way. The sound track is going to have to be changed if the new ending is going to work.

Fortunately, it is easy to change the sound track. If an unexpected background noise spoils a vocal take, the actors' lines can be re-recorded in a sound studio after the filming is completed. The actors watch the film of themselves saying the lines, and then they "lip-sync," moving their lips exactly as they did when the scene was filmed, and record them again. Of course, in the situation that Hugh and Cecily are changing, Sarah has to say new lines, so lip-syncing won't work. But that is no problem. Sarah records her new lines, and they choose a take of her in which her hair hangs over her face, so the audience can't see her lips as she speaks. Now the scene makes sense, and the ending pleases Hugh and Cecily. Careful and clever editing can produce enormous changes!

The final cut does not end the editing process, however. No television show is complete without music.

Background music, theme songs—all kinds of music are used in all kinds of television shows. Most people don't recognize background music when they hear it. It is used to enhance the mood of the scene, whether the mood is happy, sad, funny, or frightening. The theme song, on the other hand, is often instantly recognizable because it is the music that identifies the show. It is always played at the show's beginning and often at its ending, too. The theme song sets the mood of the series and gives the viewer clues as to whether the show will

original, composed especially for this show by Fred Mollin. Fred writes all kinds of music, for movies and for television. He has done the scores for the hugely popular *Friday the 13th* movies, as well as the new *Gidget* television series, and he will write the background music and the theme song for *Ramona*.

Fred said, "When I'm writing for a specific show like *Ramona*, I always work closely with the producers. I'm willing to write the kind of music they want and change what they want changed." Before he begins his work, Fred looks at videotapes of all the episodes so he will know what the series is about. After everyone decides what kind of music is needed and where it needs to be heard in the shows, Fred returns to his home to begin composing pieces that will fit the show's different moods . . . sad music for Picky-Picky's death, happy music for Aunt Bea's wedding, and so on.

"I compose and orchestrate the music at home on a computerized keyboard," Fred said, "and then I record it in a sound studio on the Kurzweil Music System. The Kurzweil is a computerized keyboard system that turns natural sounds into digital sounds. It isn't a synthesizer; it naturally reproduces any sound known to man—from birds chirping to tires squealing."

Fred uses the Kurzweil to reproduce the sounds of all the different instruments he uses in his compositions. When all the sections—flute, clarinet, piano, bass—are recorded, he is ready to mix their sounds together so the finished music will sound as if it is being played

be a comedy, a mystery, or a drama.

Sometimes television producers will acquire the rights to music that has already been composed and use it for their television show. However, *Ramona*'s music will be

by a full orchestra.

As he listens to the final orchestration, Fred makes adjustments. If the piano is too loud, he softens it. Violins too soft? He can make them louder. When the sound is exactly as he wants it, the score is put on audio music reels that are synchronized with the film.

At last, the final cut of *Ramona* is ready for sound editing. The sound editor works like the film editor. If one scene is good visually but an actor has mispronounced a word or delivered a line better in another take, the sound from the "good" voice take can be dubbed into the better visual take, resulting in a scene that both looks and sounds great! If the sound in a particular take is really bad, the actor can come into the studio and record his or her lines over again. Then the recording will be dubbed into the original sound track. The sound editor adds sound effects, too. To do this he watches a videotape of the show, and when dogs bark, cars start, eggs crack, or forks clatter he adds the appropriate sound at precisely the right moment.

Finally, the sound mixer takes all the audio elements of the film—the sound effects, the music, the dialogue of the actors—mixes them all together, and attaches the final audio tape onto the film exactly where it is supposed to be.

After over two years of hard work, the ten episodes of *Ramona* are finally ready to be shown on television. But without an audience to watch, all this work means nothing.

C · H · A · P · T · E · R   E · I · G · H · T

DON'T TOUCH THAT DIAL!

Most people who do something creative like painting pictures, writing books, or composing music want others to look at their pictures, read their books, or listen to their music. The people who create television shows are no different. They want people to watch the shows they've created, and they know that there is a lot of competition among the various networks and cable channels for each viewer's attention. So part of the postproduction process for any show includes promotion.

Atlantis Films will promote this series in North and South America. Revcom will promote it in Europe, and PBS will promote it in the United States. *Ramona* will also be seen in Australia and Japan, to name just a few foreign markets. Television stations in all these countries will do some kind of advertising and promotion to build their audience for the show.

In the United States, all the PBS stations will receive a press kit that includes photographs of Sarah, Lori, Barry, and Lynda; summaries of all ten shows; and short thirty- to sixty-second videotapes, called promos, of different scenes. The promos will have spaces for each local station to indicate the time that it will show the series. Even if the network decides to air it during prime time, the period between 8:00 and 11:00 P.M. when most Americans watch television, the local stations do not have to show *Ramona* then if they don't want to.

There will be interviews in the newspapers with Sarah and Lori, and television writers from across the country will be invited to PBS's Press Fair, where all the new shows on that network will be shown.

Television critics watch the new shows and publish reviews of them in newspapers and magazines such as *TV Guide*. A review is an article that says what a critic likes—or doesn't like—about a show. The critic comments on how the show was directed, how the sets looked, how the actors performed, and how entertaining or informative the show was. After the critic has talked about all the elements that make up a television show, he or she will make a recommendation about whether you, the viewer, should spend your time watching it.

Television broadcasting began as an experiment in 1929 when RCA installed 150 television sets in homes scattered around New York City and broadcast *Felix the Cat*. Those 150 sets have now grown to 156 *million* in the United States alone. America's children watch a combined total of 90 *billion* hours of television a year.

Since 1929, all kinds of television networks—commercial, cable, and public service—have sprung up like toadstools after a rain. Today, with 315 million television sets in the world, programs are broadcast in every country that has electricity. Television is a powerful method of communication, as powerful as books, music, art, or theater. And like those other art forms, when its shows are produced carefully and thoughtfully, television can teach us, entertain us, and remind us all of what is truly important in life.

RAMONA

A Revcom presentation

Based on the books by
Beverly Cleary

Produced by
Atlantis Films Limited

in collaboration with
Lancit Media Productions

Produced in association with Revcom Television
Michel Noll
Helene Fatou
Lee Polk
and
Bayerischer Rundfunk

With the assistance of the
Corporation for Public Broadcasting

Produced with the participation of
CHCH Television

Created for television by
Cecily Truett and Hugh Martin

Executive Producers for Atlantis Films
Michael MacMillan and Seaton McLean

Executive in Charge of Production for Lancit Media
Larry Lancit

Co-Executive Producers for Lancit Media
Hugh Martin and Cecily Truett

CAST

The Quimbys

Ramona	Sarah Polley
Beezus	Lori Chodos
Dory	Lynda Mason Green
Bob	Barry Flatman

Adults

Mrs. Whaley	Jayne Eastwood
Mrs. Larson	Nerene Virgin
Aunt Bea	Kirsten Bishop
Uncle Hobart	Barclay Hope
Grandma Kemp	Helen Hughes
Grandpa Day	Bernard Behrens
Mr. X	Tony Van Bridge
Waitress	Elizabeth Lennie
Maitre d'	Paul Jolicoeur
Michel	Tony Nardi
Beautician	Karen Holness
Doctor	Diane Polley
Nurse	Laurel Bresnahan

Children

Howie	Bobby Becken
Yard Ape	Marlow Vella
Marsha	Kerry Segal
Susan	Nicole Lyn
Tommy	Benjamin Barrett
Willa-Jean	Norma Reid

CREW

Producer Kim Todd
Director Randy Bradshaw
Director of Photography Douglas Kiefer, c.s.c.
Music Fred Mollin
Story Editor Ellis Weiner
Stories adapted by Ellis Weiner, Mark Saltzman,
Sid Fleischman, Ellen Schecter,

Art Director Mark Eisman
Editors Peter Grundy
First Assistant Director Sally Paterson, Lara Mazur
Unit Manager Erika Zborowsky
Second Assistant Director John Calvert
Continuity Frank Siracusa
Production Coordinator Madeleine Duff
Series Consultant Gillian Helfield
Production Consultant Bill Seigler
Focus Puller Gillian Spencer
Clapper Loaders Cathy Robertson
Joel D. Guthro
Cudah Andarawewa

Location Sound Mixer John J. Thomson
Boom Operator Martin Lacroix
Assistant Art Director Angus McCallum
Set Decorator Robert Bartman
Property Master Jeffrey A. Melvin
Set Dresser Lloyd Brown
Assistant Props Carolyn Loucks
Head Carpenter David Hamayda
Set Construction Edge & Bratton
Scenic Artists Nick Kosonic
Martin Mobbs

Wardrobe Designer Maya Mani
Wardrobe Assistant Mia Sturup
Hairdresser Jocelyn MacDonald
Make-up Artist Barbara Szablowski
Gaffer Gary Phipps
Best Boy Harold D. Stroud
Electric Tom Durnan
Generator Operator Roger Bowden

Key Grip Mark Silver
Best Boy Grip Ian Henderson
Production Accountant Joan Scarrow
Assistant to Accountant Solange Murciano
Dialogue Coach Jan Green
Tutor Laurel Bresnahan
Transportation Coordinator G. Kris Hawthorne
Stills Photographer Marni Grossman
Publicity Jeremy Katz
Trainee Assistant Director Jill Compton
Office Production Assistants Anthony Kadak
Lori Isenbaum

Art Department Trainee Ray Lorenz
Craft Service Amerind Day
Cat Wrangler Laura Fisher
Catering Blue Heron Catering
Casting Arlene Berman Casting
Extras Casting Rose Lewis Casting
Casting Consultant Darlene Kaplan
Postproduction Coordinator Daphne Ballon
Postproduction Assistants John Harcourt
Roberta Kipp

Sound Effects Editor Arnie Stewart
Dialogue Editors Marta Sternberg
Dale Sheldrake
Assistant Picture Editors Dawn Higgins
Gloria Thorsteinson

Assistant Sound Editor/ADR Michele Cook
Second Assistant Editor Brett C. Sullivan
Editing Apprentice Thor Henrikson
Rerecording Mixers Wally Weaver
Daniel Pellerin

Foley Artist Andy Malcolm
Lab and mixing PFA Film & Video
Negative cutting May Bischof
Opticals Film Opticals, Toronto
Titles Metromedia